The Life You Want

The Life You Want

The Key to a Happy and Fulfilling Life

Brigitte Novalis

Novalis Press

Published by Novalis Press

ISBN 978-1-944870-23-2

Typesetting services by BOOKOW.COM

I thank you, Torsten Zimmer,
for your valuable artistic
and linguistic advice!

Contents

Preface   **1**

What is the Key to a Happy and Fulfilling Life?   1

1	**The Life You Want**	**5**
2	**How do You Want Your Life to Be?**	**17**
3	**One Thing I Really Want**	**31**
4	**Romantic Relationships**	**47**
5	**So, You Think I'm Good?**	**57**
6	**All People and the Vibrating Universe**	**73**
7	**The Ocean of Well-Being**	**89**

8	Small Children and Freedom of Choice	97
9	The Golden Gate	111
10	Is Life Fair?	123
11	Promise	133

Preface

What is the Key to a Happy and Fulfilling Life?

Do you know that you can live the life you want? *You can*—if you know how to go about it. If you truly want to live a life that is brighter, richer, more peaceful, more joyful and—if you wish—*more playful* than the life you live right now, you may have to make some changes.

You know that, right? If you continue doing what you have been doing, and thinking what you have been thinking, you will get what you got before—the same old, over and over.

On the other hand, the life you truly want for yourself is waiting for you, bright and beautiful. The good news is that *you* are the one who can make it happen. If you are asking yourself how, this book will answer that question for you *if you truly desire it*.

Oh, I better introduce myself. My name is Brigitte Novalis, and I am an intuitive healer and a therapist. As a clinical hypnotherapist and a neurolinguistic therapist, I have worked to heal the minds of my clients, their deeper, subconscious minds. As a Reiki Master, I have learned to work with energies as well.

Once my clients have solved their pressing problems, I like to ask them, "Are you ready for the next step?" Usually, they are stunned.

"Next step? What do you mean by 'next step'?" And I ask them, "How do you want your life to be?"

For many, this is shocking. They have never thought what *they want* really matters. They have only ever known a life of being pushed around by circumstances. But this is not reality. There is more to life than being pushed around. Life can be enjoyable and fulfilling. In fact, it is meant to be that way.

By the way, I did not plan on writing this book. As it happened, one evening I was compelled to open a blank Word document and to type the words: *The Life You Want*. "Funny," I thought, "this looks like the title of a new book," but I had no clue how to go about writing it.

As I gazed at the blinking cursor, I heard a voice in my mind, the slightly irritated voice of a young man. "The Life You Want?" he asked, "What kind of title is that?"

And then an answer came to my mind, and in that way, a dialogue unfolded in intervals day by day, week by week. From where? I cannot pinpoint it. This book seems to have a life of its own.

I invite you to engage in the dialogue. Imagine your own voice as you read. Play an active part! As you use my transformative healing techniques and witness the flood of questions, answers, hopes, and insights, your life will change for the better.

You will find the key to a happy and fulfilling life. You will find *the* most important single thing you can do for yourself to start living the life you want. Do you want to know what that looks like?

Read on.

Chapter 1

The Life You Want

And so goes the dialogue:

"'The life you want?' What kind of title is that?

"Did anybody ask me how I wanted my life to be? **Want?** *They did not even ask me* **if I** *want to live this life, let alone* **how I want to live it.**

"Who does? We are born unasked, before that, conceived unasked. Then we are here, naked, hungry, and helpless. Did we want that? To be born into an unknown environment and be so dependent on others? I don't think so."

"Wait, wait. Hold your horses. Yes, you chose to live this life. You doubt it? You are even upset about it?

"Let me ask you, don't you know that you want to be here, to live this life? If you are really honest with yourself, don't you know it deep down? Don't you feel it?"

"Well, yes, in a way. But what does it matter?"

"What does it matter? *You* matter. You are unique. There is no one in the entire world exactly like you. You are unique, important, and good."

"Important? How can you say that? Right now, we have more than seven billion people on Earth. Seven billion. There are so many people they are like sand in the desert, and you tell me that I am important?"

"Forget about others for a moment. Just concentrate on yourself. Be aware of yourself. You look out of your eyes; you hear with your ears; you touch with your hands—are these experiences important to you or not? Is what you feel right now important to you or not?"

"What does it matter?"

"Does it matter to you?"

"I guess. Yes. But that does not make me feel any better. If you knew how many mornings I wake up feeling so dreadful and how many nights I can't fall asleep because I feel so lonely and empty..."

"I know."

"How can you know that? You don't know my life."

"More or less, we all go through similar experiences. To a certain degree, we all suffer from a sad heart or a lonely heart or an empty heart, unless..."

"Unless what?"

"Unless we heal it."

"Heal it? How do we do that?"

"By filling our hearts with love. Some have always done so, some learn to do it easily, others find it difficult to do; the most important thing is—it works."

"You must be kidding."

"Not at all. Are you interested in learning how to do this?"

"If it does not take too much time."

"Okay. Here it goes."

Imagine the little baby that you once were, about a year old. Imagine holding your baby self in your arms and love this baby.

Love the baby self with all your heart. Talk to him gently and kindly.

Tell your baby that he is precious and unique and that he deserves all the happiness in the world.

Love your baby self until you feel good and happy and the baby in your arms, which you once were, will also seem to be happy.

"That's it? That will make me feel better? I just imagine something and it makes me feel better? That's weird."

"Well, is it really? If you imagine your boss getting angry with you and firing you, this thought can stress you out. You can imagine all kinds of trouble and feel bad afterwards, or you can imagine pleasant events and feel good afterwards. You do this all the time, imagining things in your mind. Unfortunately, people usually imagine all kinds of difficulties. They worry and worry, so their lives become more and more troubled."

"But this still seems far-fetched. I imagine holding myself as a kid, and I feel better afterwards?"

"That was only the first part of it. What I suggested is that you imagine holding your baby self in your arms *and* love him. You love the little one you once were. This means, of course, that you love yourself. That makes all the difference in your life. You see, for many people it *seems* so difficult to love or appreciate themselves. I have met people who don't like themselves, even some who despise themselves. Do you think that a person like that can enjoy life?"

"You've got a point there. But still, do you really believe that when I imagine holding myself as a kid—"

"And *love* him…"

"And love him, that all the sadness and loneliness in my life will be gone?"

"If you do it often enough, it will dramatically change your life.

"Do you want to give it a try? Yes? Good. Now, please hold your little baby and love your baby self with all your heart. When you feel good, and the little one also seems content, let me know."

* * *

"There is a problem. I tried to love him, but I can't feel it. It doesn't work for me."

"If you can't feel love, then you can start by silently telling him in your mind, 'I love you. I love you, little one. I love you.'

"You say it over and over. And then you start feeling good and then better and better."

"Well, I can do that, but I don't understand how it could work. I say something and then I feel different?"

"When you say something out loud or quietly in your mind, and you say it repeatedly, it changes the way you feel because energy follows thought."

"Huh, that's weird.
'Energy follows thought.'
What kind of energy?"

"Emotional energy. Emotions are what you feel inside when you think of something you love or fear. Emotions are energy.

"E-motion = energy in motion.

"Ready to go?"

"Wait. Give me a moment."

* * *

"Can I ask you a question? It seems like my little boy doesn't want me to hold him. I don't think he likes me."

"Be patient. He must have been lonely and upset for a long time. Be gentle with him, talk to him from your heart, and love him."

"This is weird, loving the baby I once was."

"Do it just the same."

* * *

"Hmm. Interesting. It feels nice, actually. Who would have guessed? Not me. And he seemed to like me by the end. That is good, isn't it?"

"Very good. Would you like to add a little something to wrap it up, so to speak?"

"Go ahead. Tell me."

"I want you to imagine something again. This time, I want you to imagine going back in time. Now you are the baby boy. You see or maybe hear your parents, or maybe you are just aware of your parents. Your parents play with you, talk to you, and make you laugh. Take your time imagining this, and let me know when you are done."

"I can't imagine that. They weren't like that at all."

"It doesn't matter. Do your best to use your imagination."

"You mean you want me to pretend that they played with me and tickled me?"

"Yes, do your best. Make it really good. You can do it."

"If you insist."

* * *

"Well, how do you feel now?"

"Funny, I feel good. Really good. Thank you."

Chapter 2

How do You Want Your Life to Be?

"So, how do you want your life to be?"

"Good question! Let me see... I want a life without anger or fear. I want a life without war and strife. I want a life where I don't need to worry about anything. I want..."

"Hold on. The question was 'How do you want your life to be?'"

"I told you, and I am not even done."

"No, you did not tell me how you want your life to be. You told me how you want your life NOT to be."

"Ah, right. Well, that's tricky. How do I want my life to be? Happy? I think happy would be good. And healthy and without sorrows—"

"Wait. You did it again. You said 'without sorrows.'"

"What's wrong with that? I don't want sorrows. No one would ask for sorrows. That is perfectly reasonable."

"It seems perfectly reasonable, but when you think of what you *don't* want, that's what you have in mind. As you think of *not* having sorrows, you have sorrows in mind."

"How do you figure?"

"That's how the mind works. You doubt it? Okay, let me give you an example. You are good at imagining things, right? So, please *don't* image a *pink dinosaur*. What are you thinking about?"

"A pink dinosaur. Why is that?"

"That is because your mind, especially your deeper mind, can't imagine *no* or *not*. So if you say or imagine "*no* pink dinosaur" a pink dinosaur is on your mind."

"Right, but what do you suggest I think about then? Don't tell me that you expect me to want sorrows?"

"No, the opposite actually! When you think about sorrows, you have sorrows in mind.

Even if you think that you don't want sorrows, you're thinking about sorrows. When you think about happiness, you have happiness in mind.

"When you think about disease, you have disease in mind. Even if you think that you don't want to be sick, you're thinking about disease. On the other hand, when you think about perfect health, you have perfect health in mind. When you think about financial stress, you have financial stress in mind. Even if you think that you hate money problems, you have money problems in mind. On the other hand, when you think about abundance, you have abundance in mind."

"Enough. Okay, I get it. The question is, why does it matter what I have in mind?"

"It matters because you attract into your life

the situations, events, and things you think about, consciously or unconsciously."

"That's funny. So, when I think about a pink dinosaur, I will end up finding a pink dinosaur in my backyard?"

"Maybe, if you travel back in time millions of years."

"Now, seriously. When I think of something, it comes to me?"

"More or less, yes."

"What do you mean by 'more or less'? Either it is a rule or not. Do you mean there are exceptions? And if so, what do they depend on?"

"They depend on the intensity of your thoughts and accompanying emotions. If something goes wrong and you say to yourself, "Well, it's all downhill from here," but it is just a fleeting thought, something that you are not serious about and don't pursue longer, then things will continue as they are.

"However, if you are in a black mood, choose to remember trouble from the past, and imagine more trouble in the future, you will get angry and scared then things *will* most likely go downhill."

"It all seems so weird. I mean, I've never thought this way. Here I was minding my own business and thinking my thoughts, and now you come and tell me that it matters what I think. Why are my thoughts so important?"

"When you put your attention on something, you give it energy. When you let your mind run wild, thinking of something pleasant one moment and worrying about something the next, you can expect a little bit of this and a little bit of that; something pleasant happens and then a little later something upsetting happens.

"On the other hand, if you have a positive plan that you feel good about and think of often with intention, then your plan often times becomes reality."

"When I hear you say it, it makes sense but I still don't understand how what I think in my own mind and body can have an effect on something or someone outside of me—out there."

"It works because your thoughts do not only happen within your head. You transmit them like a TV tower transmits electro-magnetic waves that are translated into pictures and sounds by your TV set at home. Your thoughts and emotions radiate out of you as if you were a big antenna."

"So, when I think of good things, good things come to me, and when I think of bad things, bad things come to me? How does that work?"

"Because of the universal Law of Resonance. It means 'like attracts like.' For example, if you have two string instruments lying on your table, a guitar and a violin, and you pluck the A-string of the violin, the A-string of the guitar will also vibrate while the other strings will remain still."

"So, you are saying 'good vibrates with good and bad vibrates with bad'?"

"You got it!"

"Let's just say you are right. If so, that is big, really big. I never looked at life from that angle. In a way, it makes me feel uncomfortable. I kind of feel overwhelmed."

"It is natural to feel overwhelmed when we consider the broader pictures of life. Any big change in our lives, for that matter, can make us feel uncomfortable, even if it is a change for the better. We tend to cling to the small, safe nests we build for ourselves.

"May I come back to the question of how you want your life to be?"

"I'd like it to be happy, prosperous, healthy, and successful. Yes, that sums it up nicely."

"It sums it up, yes, but could you be a little more specific?"

"Why? That covers what I want in life—happiness, health, wealth, and success. That is exactly what I want."

"I wouldn't call it exact at all. Those are only general ideas. If you want to have something, you have to be more specific.

"Let me give you an example. Imagine that one morning the doorbell rings, and as you open the front door, you see three elegantly dressed men at your doorstep who present you with a document that says you have been selected to be the VIP customer of a newly opened superstore. They explain that you can get anything you want from that superstore for free. You only have to tell them what you want. That would be nice, right?

"Now these men ask you, 'What would you like to have?'

"As it is early morning and you have not had breakfast, you struggle to come up with something important. Finally, you say, 'Some new furniture.' And they ask politely, 'What kind of furniture?'

"You think of the shabby furniture in the living room and say, 'Something for the living room.'

"They reply, 'What exactly do you need for the living room?'

"And you say, 'Something to sit on and something to put things on. It must be practical and of good quality.'

"They ask you again, 'Yes, we will do that, but can you please tell us what kind of furniture you want for the living room?'

"Now you get slightly impatient and say, 'I told you already.'

"And they ask you in return, 'Are you sure you don't want to give us more details?'

"And you say, 'Yes, I'm sure. Anything new will be fine.' They leave and you have breakfast.

"In the afternoon when you come home from work, you see a big truck parked in your driveway, and you have to park in the street. 'What are you doing in my driveway?' you ask the truck driver.

"He climbs down and greets you politely. 'Delivering your furniture,' he says. He and his colleague follow you into the house and glance at your living room.

"'This will be easy,' the truck driver says. 'We'll be done in no time. Just leave it to us. Soon you will be able to enjoy your new furniture.'

"At this moment you'd like to cancel the whole thing, but there is the big truck, and there are these two helpful men that you don't want to disappoint. So you go to the kitchen and put on the radio, whistling along with the tunes as you start to prepare supper. However, you can't ignore all the sounds of shoveling, carrying, and dismantling coming from the living room. You eat and read the paper, and still they are working hard. Finally, it becomes quiet. There is a soft knock at the door. As you open it, the two guys, sweaty and content, smile at you and present you with a list.

"'So, what do you think?' the driver asks, sweeping his hand around the room.

"'Would you please sign the delivery slip at the bottom to acknowledge that you have received them?'

"As you walk into the living room, you have

to swallow hard. Yes, the furniture there is practical and of good quality. At the center is a large oak table with six chestnut chairs. You see a mahogany wardrobe at one side and a large black leather sofa at the other side flanked by Chippendalestyle side tables. There is more furniture, which must serve a good purpose and is certainly of good quality, but oh, how awful this room looks. Nothing fits together. You feel like fainting and close your eyes.

'"What have you done?' you whisper weakly.

'"We delivered what you ordered. Please enjoy your new furniture.'

"All right, all right. I get the picture."

Chapter 3

One Thing I Really Want

"Okay, so I'll be more specific. One thing I want is to have happy relationships. Let's start with my father, although I don't know if I should put him on my wish list —nothing will change my old man."

"This is not about changing him; this is about having a better relationship with him."

"You mean the relationship on my end?"

"That's what I have in mind."

"Excuse me, but I am not the one who causes trouble. It's my father. You can't imagine how much I feared him and his anger when I was a child. No matter what I did, it was not good enough for him. There were times when I was so close to running away from home, so close. The only reason I didn't was the even greater fear of what he would do to me if the police brought me back. You have no idea what I went through."

"What about today? Are you still in contact with your father?"

"Yes, some phone calls, some visits. I really dread going there for holidays."

"But you still go there? Then there must be some good in this relationship or else you would not visit with him."

"No, it is just horrible from beginning to end."

"How long have you been feeling this way?"

"For as long as I can remember."

"Do you want to carry this anger and fear along with you for the rest of your life? You see, all the things that were unpleasant and upsetting in the past are upsetting now, and will be in the future, unless you dissolve them."

"Are you saying that this dreadful feeling that I get when I think of my father will stay with me for the rest of my life? What if I don't think of him?"

"It is a good idea not to dwell on the past but instead to live your life in the present moment and be as happy as you can be right now. However, oftentimes everyday situations can trigger old hurt and the painful emotions flare up again. Even if you push the old hurt deeper down into the background of your emotions, and you don't feel it as acutely as before, it is still there; it colors your expectations and limits your freedom."

"What do you mean by that?"

"Let's say you meet an older gentleman—he could be your boss or the father of your girlfriend—and maybe he has grey hair or mannerisms like your father or shares one of your father's hobbies, and you are reminded of your father. So, when you meet this old gentleman, you cringe inside. Without being fully aware of it, you expect him to be as judgmental as your father has been.

"You find it difficult to like this man because

your old emotions are in the way. Such an automatic reaction can hinder your ability to approach him with an open mind and an open heart. He might be the kindest of men, but you don't give yourself the chance to find out."

"And you say that we can dissolve these blocks in our mind that we carry around with us?"

"Sure. Would you like to do that?"

"You mean, right here and now?"

"Now is the best of times."

"Well, I don't think I am prepared for something so far-reaching. I might not remember all the awful things that happened back then."

"You don't have to. Just relax, close your eyes, and feel that dreadful feeling."

"Okay."

"To start, get comfortable in your chair and close your eyes. In your mind, go backwards in time to a moment when you were very angry with your father.

"As soon as you feel this anger, stop picturing your father; don't argue with him in your mind. Keep your mind as quiet as you can. Just be aware of those horrible feelings."

"That feels awful. I don't like feeling this."

"Shush, trust me. Just do it. And now become more and more aware of this anger as something that is happening inside of you right now. Stop identifying with it. Step out of the feeling and observe it. Observe it with kindness.

"Now, imagine that you hold this anger like you were holding the little baby you once were. Even make it look like your baby self, only with a different color so that you can distinguish them. Maybe this anger baby self is blue or green or orange. What color would you like him to have?"

"Well, let's see. Orange maybe?"

"Orange is good. Okay. Hold him tenderly and love him. Comfort him. Speak gently to him in your mind, and let him know that there is nothing to fear, that he is safe with you and that you love him no matter what. Love him as much as you are able to love someone. After a while, you will not feel anger but love. Let me know when that happens."

* * *

"Well, are you feeling some relief? Is the feeling getting lighter? Good. Just continue to feel the feeling and let me know when you feel a change."

* * *

"Yes, you are right. I feel different. I don't feel that awful feeling anymore. It feels as if it doesn't matter anymore. That's cool. Thank you. What is next? How do I get that great relationship with my father?"

"Not so fast. First, I want you to get up to speed with your energies. I want you to love your little baby boy again as you did earlier. This time, not your orange anger baby but your baby self."

"You mean, holding the little kid I was in my arms and loving him?"

"That's right."

"I still find that's a weird thing to do, pretending to love the little kid I was."

"Wait a minute! I said nothing about pretending. I said 'loving.' So, please, love him as much as you are able to love someone."

* * *

"You're smiling. How do you feel?"

"Good. Really good. Now, what about the good relationship with my father?"

"Can you tell me anything nice or good about your father?"

"Well, let me see... He takes good care of the house. He is always repairing something or another. Oh yeah, he is also a great gardener."

"That is something to build on. I would like you to close your eyes so that you can imagine things better. Now, imagine visiting your parents and walking around the house and through the garden with your father. Appreciate the good work he has done and is still doing. Maybe you also ask him some questions about what he is planning to do in the near future. Picture yourself and him in his garden and see how both of you show your best behavior."

"You are asking a lot of me."

"Just do it, and give it some time. When you feel good about the situation, you may open your eyes again."

* * *

"That was not so bad, really. So, in my mind I can get along with him okay, but what about real life?"

"In real life, not to say that what you did just now in your mind was not real life, you do the same. As you appreciate what you can appreciate about him, you feel better in this relationship. As long as you hold onto that appreciation, you feel good."

"But what if he pesters me about something? What do I do then?"

"Maybe he does not pester you so much when he feels your good vibes towards him."

"Yes, maybe. But what about my mother? As soon as I sit at the dinner table, she

starts complaining about how expensive everything is and how people are no longer as kind as they were when she was younger. She goes on and on about it! And then she asks me if I've met a decent girl and when I will get married because she wants to have grandchildren. When I ask her to lay off, she always says that it is only for my own good."

"How do you feel about it?"

"Lousy."

"Please, feel that lousy feeling. You know how to do it by now. Once you feel the bad feeling, stop picturing the situation and stop arguing in your mind about it. Just feel the feeling and then make it into your anger baby, the orange baby. Love him as much as you are able to love someone. After a while, you will not feel anger but love. Let me know when that happens."

* * *

"Well, I have to say, it really makes a difference. I feel much better. But how do I get a better relationship with my mother?

"You use your creative mind again. Close your eyes and imagine going into the future and seeing your father and your mother, and all of you are friendly and open-minded."

"I wish. And when I am really there, what would I do?"

"When you are in the kitchen, and you all eat your mother's soup, and she keeps on complaining how expensive everything is, you say, 'Hey, Mom, your soup is so good. How do you do it? I'd really like to have the recipe.'

"She will feel pleased about making a good soup, and she will tell you how she makes it.

Imagine her writing the recipe down for you with a smile on her face. She can't complain because she can't feel good about her soup-making abilities and feel bad about something else at the same time.

"In general, when you talk kindly to her, she feels better. By the way, not only people want to be appreciated but also dogs and cats and birds and trees and flowers, in fact, every living being. As you appreciate your mother, she feels better and starts thinking slightly better about herself and about you, too. As a consequence of that, your visit will be more pleasant."

"I can see that, but what can I do if they start bickering again later on?"

"In that case, as you eat the soup, you close your ears to their bickering and look out of the window. Say to yourself, 'It's a beautiful day, just right for a walk through the old neighborhood.' And when you are done eating, you go for a walk."

Chapter 4

Romantic Relationships

"Now that I'm starting to feel better about myself, for some reason I'm starting to think about better relationships, but what about relationships that don't exist?"

"What do you mean by 'relationships that don't exist'?"

"Well, I would really like to have a girlfriend, a girl I could be happy with, but

I'm not dating anyone right now. Can I do something now to help my future relationship before I have it?"

"Great question! Absolutely! So, right now you are not dating?"

"Nope."

"But you have dated before, right?"

"Well, sure, not just once."

"What happened? Why are you no longer in a relationship?"

"You know, they all started out so nicely, but after a time they just stopped being easy and fun and become too much work. They always ended badly, and it was so upsetting. Now I am a little apprehensive about relationships. I don't want

to go through the turmoil again. First you think everything is fine, and you are happy, and then it goes downhill and becomes really sad. Although I would really like to have a good relationship with a nice girl, I don't know how to make it work."

"As you said, at one time you were happy with your girlfriend. The relationship you were in seemed to be so easy-going and pleasant. But, as time went by, little things got in the way. She did not seem to care as much as earlier. Maybe she started being late for dates, or she did not listen to you, or she was just downright grumpy.

"Then, when you thought of her, you remembered this unpleasant behavior towards you, and you felt apprehensive. You started to expect to be hurt, and so you invited more of this into your life. As Kahlil Gibran says in his book *Sand and Foam*, 'We choose our joys and sorrows long before we experience them.'

"Excuse me, but that makes no sense. Who would choose sorrows?"

"Have you forgotten? When you dwell on sorrows of the past or the present, or even potential future ones, you draw sorrows into your life experience."

"Ah, yes, I remember. Anyway, is this Kahlil Gibran saying that I have to feel good before I can experience the good that I want? I have to enjoy the cake before I can eat it, so to speak? That sounds silly."

"Don't you think it makes a difference if you think, 'Ah, I am looking forward to that birthday party where they serve all that delicious cake,' rather than 'Ugh, I hate going to these parties. My stomach already hurts thinking of the sugary cakes they'll probably serve there."

"You have a point, but what does this have to do with my girlfriend?"

"Right, let's go back to your relationship and the distance you felt with your girlfriend. Let's say the distance started with you. When you saw her, she would sense the distance you felt; it radiated out of you. At first, it was probably not much. There were still more pleasant things in the relationship than unpleasant things.

"However, as you continued to have more unpleasant thoughts and feelings towards your girlfriend, she became more and more aware of your inner critique. Her reaction to them became stronger. Over time, both of you began to interact out of hurt and anger instead of out of kindness and love. As a consequence, the relationship went downhill."

"I agree. I never looked at my relationship from that angle, but you have described it very well. The question is, how can I change that?"

"You can change it by deliberately looking for the good in her. By paying attention to everything she does that you might consider good."

"Do you know what you're asking? If you knew how my last girlfriend behaved at the end, you would understand that there wasn't much good to be found in her."

"I admit that at times we feel that there is not much good in another person, but that is not true.

"As long as you are still in a relationship, and you want an improvement, stretch yourself. Find something, anything, nice and pleasant in her behavior and focus on it. Look for a gentle smile and a kind remark, even though it might be difficult.

"As you start feeling this newly discovered pleasant feeling for her, it radiates out of you. She will feel it and respond to it positively. In this way, you put your relationship back on an uphill path."

"Well, if I am fortunate enough to have a relationship again, I can do that. But what can I do now?"

"First of all, it is a good idea to let go of the old feelings of hurt and anger because they are still inside of you. By now you know how to do that. Feel the feeling, but don't picture the situation. Stop your thoughts. Just be present with your emotions. Imagine holding the orange baby self, the anger baby, in your arms.

"Hold him tenderly and love him. Comfort him. Speak to him gently in your mind and let him know that there is nothing to fear, that he is safe with you, and that you love him no matter what. Love him as you did earlier. After a while, you will not feel anger but love. Let me know when that happens."

* * *

"This is really surprising. I am not angry any more. It feels as if the old quarrels don't really matter anymore. In fact, I don't feel anything about her. Is that good?"

"Better than being resentful, don't you think? You can also choose to think kindly of her. If you wish, you can close your eyes for a moment and imagine going back in time. Picture the two of you standing next to one another. Now see or feel how you smile at each other as you say goodbye."

* * *

"How do you feel?"

"Don't laugh at me, but I feel weird. Like I'm a good person."

"You *are* a good person, aren't you starting to get that?"

Chapter 5

So, You Think I'm Good?

"I still have to think about what you said earlier. So, you think I am good?"

"Yes, I do."

"How can you say that? You hardly know me. If you did, you might not like me at all."

"Would it matter to you?"

"Yes, it matters. I want you to like me. To tell you the truth, I think I'd want almost everyone to like me. You know, some times when I meet people and get the feeling they don't approve of me, it makes me feel sad."

"May I ask you if you approve of yourself?"

"Well, I don't dislike myself. I think I'm a pretty decent human being. I am not mean or cruel or irresponsible or anything like that. But there are times when I think I could have done better in certain situations, which makes me really angry at myself. Sometimes, I'm even ashamed of myself. It's a rotten feeling."

"Do you think there are people who never make mistakes?"

"Maybe people like the Dalai Lama, but almost everyone makes mistakes. However, that does not stop me from feeling bad about myself when I do something wrong. And the worst part is that it comes to mind again and again. It is like having a bad tooth—your tongue has to touch it every now and then, and each time it hurts again. Do you know what I mean?"

"Oh, yes. As bad as that is, that is not even the worst part. It is even worse if those painful memories go into hiding in our mind. When that happens, we just feel bad about ourselves without even remembering where the bad feeling is coming from. Then we conclude that something must be wrong with us and that we don't deserve happiness and success."

"And if we don't know where that lousy feeling comes from, then we can't heal it, right?"

"We can always heal the past and start enjoying life again. Always."

"How would we do that without remembering what happened?"

"You are still able to feel, right? This emotion that you feel is precious. It guides you to recover and feel better again, if you just let it happen."

"Let what happen?"

"The emotion—feel what you feel. Feel it without thinking about it because your thinking just adds fuel to the fire; feel it without picturing the painful situations. Keep your mind out of it as much as you can. Feel, just feel, this uncomfortable feeling.

"Don't identify with it, however. Feel it in a way that you acknowledge that it is there; after all, you have created it. Feel it and observe it and then hold it in your arms as your baby self, only in a different color, maybe green or violet, then love it with all your heart."

"Okay, okay. I will do it, but I don't know exactly what I am supposed to be feeling."

"You will feel the jumbled feelings of not being good enough."

"And when I feel it, I make it into a green copy of my own baby self and get rid of the bad energy?"

"No, that is not what I want you to do. You can't and shouldn't get rid of your energy. What you can do is transform the negative charge of your emotional energy.

"You see, this emotion has been with you for a long time. Part of your energy is charged with the emotion of not being good enough. Does that make sense to you?"

"Not really."

"You know that the human body is complex, right? So is the mind. It might help to think of some parts of your energies as clear water, like water you see in a glass. When something bad happens in life, the energy or water gets darkened by ink. The energy is still your energy, but the ink has changed it. That's what I mean by the energy having a negative charge.

"As you love this darkened energy, you transform it into a brighter, happier energy. Love transforms it all."

"So, what am I supposed to do now? Feel the feeling of not being good enough, make it into a green copy of my baby self, and love it?"

"Yes. That would make a dramatic difference in your life."

"If you say so."

* * *

"How long am I supposed to feel this? I can hardly feel any change. This is taking forever."

"Shush. Just stay with the emotion and love that dear green baby."

* * *

"Well, I must say, it was worth the time. I still don't think I am a terribly good person, but I feel better about myself. I do.

Somehow lighter and freer. That's nice. I like that feeling.

"You might be surprised, but I still wonder why you said I am good. So you think I am good without knowing me very well?"

"Of course. Basically, human beings are good."

"Well, maybe deep, deep down somewhere. So deep down that I hardly notice it in some people.

"So, when you say I am good then you mean it in the sense that you believe somehow everybody is good? Even the blackest sheep? Is this like a blanket of benevolent feelings that you wrap around everyone? Are you saying that I am good just as a friendly, and forgive me, off-the-cuff remark?"

"You might think that you must do some good deeds in order to be good, whatever these good deeds might be. You might think that you have to prove your goodness and worthiness to yourself, to other people, or even to the world at large or to God before you can consider yourself good.

"By the way, you could pursue the issue of becoming good or worthy all your life; you will never get there. What you might get instead is a sense of self-righteousness and that, of course, leads you downhill.

"No, you don't have to prove that you are good. You are good. Goodness is your true nature."

"Nice thought, but it doesn't satisfy me. I can't grasp it. It is like a painting of a meal, all canvas and oil. No matter how hungry I am, I can't eat it. Can you help

me? I would really like to believe that I am good."

"There is only one thing you can say that is true about yourself—you exist. This observation and understanding goes along with a feeling-tone, the feeling-tone of your own being. This feeling-tone is there all your life, from birth to death and beyond. It never changes. You might call it your 'I am' feeling.

"I am wondering if you can feel it now."

"You mean, right now?"

"Indeed. Now is as good a time as any."

"Honestly, I find this difficult. It sounds silly, I know, but can you help me feel this 'I am' feeling, as you call it?"

"Easily. First, become aware of your body—where you sit, how your body rests on your chair. Feel your feet…"

"Excuse me, what do you mean by 'feel your feet'? Touching them?"

"No, feel them from the inside. Become aware of them."

"Oh boy, this is much more difficult than I thought it would be. Feeling my feet. Please give me a moment here. Feeling my feet… You'd think it would be the most natural thing in the world, to feel your feet. After all, they are part of me, but no, it's difficult. I know that I have feet but feeling them?"

"Take your time. It might help if you move your toes a bit."

* * *

"Right, I got it! Funny, it is not so different from how I felt before. I am just more aware of my feet somehow. It is a nice feeling, by the way, like being more alive. Okay. What's next?"

"Feel your breath as you breathe in and out."

"I can do that."

"Become aware of your entire body."

"I am getting there! It's easy if you know how to go about it."

"And become aware of subtle energy flows in your body."

"Do you have to make it more difficult? I was just starting to think that I am good

at this, and now you spoiled it. What kind of energies am I supposed to feel in my body?"

"Shush. Just do it. When you are able to feel your body, you can also feel your energies. Just quiet your mind and focus your attention inside of you. If you want to feel your energies, eventually you will feel them. It's natural. You can do it."

* * *

"Yes, I am beginning to feel them. It's not a

strong feeling, but I'm somehow aware of something like energy flowing through me. Funny, I did not know it was there."

"Are you ready for more?"

"You bet."

"Now become aware of an inner presence—your inner presence."

* * *

"Well, how do you feel? Are you more aware of yourself?"

"That's it! Exactly. I am more aware of myself. Of course, I always knew that I am me. That's a matter of fact, right? Who else could I be? But I hardly ever thought about it."

"Now hold that awareness of yourself in your mind."

* * *

"How does it feel?"

"It feels good."

"What about yourself? How do you feel about yourself?"

"I feel good about myself. I really do."

Chapter 6

All People and the Vibrating Universe

"Do you think it's possible to have good relationships with all people, not just family and friends?"

"What do you mean by 'all people'? Do you mean everybody on Earth, more than 7 billion people?"

"I thought of all the people in my life, like neighbors and colleagues. However, it is

*an interesting thought to have good rela-
tionships with everybody on Earth, isn't
it? Is that possible?"*

"Well, relationship means two parties—you
and one other, you and many others, you and
mankind. In a way, we have a relationship
with everyone because we are all connected.
After all, we are all human beings living on
planet Earth at this particular time. We are
one mankind, regardless of how different we
may act or look or behave, don't you agree?"

*"But we don't know everyone, right? So
how can we have a relationship with each
other?"*

"It is not an immediate and direct relationship
like your relationships with your friends. You
know your friends, at least to a certain degree,
and you experience directly how you feel when
they smile or yell at you.

"We are not aware of how all the others on planet Earth feel specifically. However, our experience of mankind is a little different than ever before—we are much more aware of what happens around the world. Tsunamis, earthquakes, hurricanes—we hear or read about them. Even if you don't read the paper, the news travels by radio, TV, internet, and word of mouth. On a certain level, people from all over the world know each other and are compassionate with each other. This compassion is like stars rising, rays of hope in the darkness."

"Yes, and people send money to help the victims of catastrophes. All the richer countries in the world do that."

"Not just the wealthy countries; the generosity comes from countries with all levels of income. It is moving to learn how populations who struggle still manage to give help to wealthier nations.

"They don't think so much of the rich and mighty nation where the catastrophe happened but of its citizens who are in pain, fear, and need. They probably think, 'They are just like us, struggling and suffering like us, so let's help them.' I think that this is a very good relationship."

"Absolutely, that is good. However, it is a secondhand relationship. We don't feel what is going on, right? We have to read or hear about it."

"If you become more sensitive—and we can all become more sensitive—as you wake up, you might feel that something has happened. You can feel the turmoil and anguish, although you don't know exactly what has happened. Again, this awareness **can** be learned. Later you may hear the specific news of what happened."

"The difference is, I can talk to my friend if he is in trouble and help and comfort him. However, I can't do that for people who live on the other side of the planet."

"While it is true that you can't hug and talk to them, you can help and comfort them."

"Help, yes, but how do I comfort them?"

"Good question. Whether they are right in front of you or thousands of miles away, you can think of them kindly and wish them well. In your imagination, you can hug them. You can imagine seeing them smile again, reunite with their family members, and build up their homes again. In your thoughts, you can tell them, 'I know you are brave and good, and you will find your way through this. You are loved and you deserve it.' In your imagination, you can see them thrive, and that will truly help them."

"*That will help them? How?*"

"Remember that we talked about our thoughts not just 'happening' in our head? I described how they are energies that we send out and that can be received by others."

"*Yes, I remember that we talked about how it relates to my family and friends. At the time, it made sense to me, but right now I'm at a loss. How can such flimsy things like thoughts possibly affect people thousands of miles away?*"

"In order to answer that question, let's philosophize for a moment. Are you okay with that?"

"Fire away!"

"You have heard of Albert Einstein and his famous formula, right?"

"Of course, who hasn't?"

"May I ask you, do you remember the formula?"

"Give me a moment. I have seen it many times... Right, here it goes:

$$e = mc^2.$$

"And I know what it means—energy (e) equals mass (m) multiplied by the speed of light (c) squared. Not just by the speed of light but the speed of light multiplied by the speed of light. Impressive, right?"

"Absolutely. What Einstein stated is that energy and matter are two different expressions of the same universal stuff, which is a primal energy. Amazing, right? And even more amazing? We are all composed of this universal energy."

"Honestly, I can't imagine that. What about atoms? We learned in school that everything is made up of atoms, and atoms are tiny blobs of matter, right?"

"Yes, according to the Bohr model of the atom, but in the quantum mechanical model we have a nucleus surrounded by a cloud of electrons. These electrons are spinning constantly around the nucleus, and so the atom is vibrating within itself. All things vibrate, because all things are composed of atoms.

"Here is another fascinating thought. If we imagine an enlarged atom the size of our solar system and compare this atom with our solar system, we would see that the electrons in an atom are as far from the nucleus as the planets are from the sun. The atom is 99.9% space, not really a blob of matter."

"But if matter is mostly space, then why do we see and feel anything as solid?"

"Because our own bodies are also composed of atoms, as is the chair you sit on. Amazingly, an atom is basically nothing but energy and information."

"Hmm… I didn't realize that before, even though I knew we were made up of atoms.

It's strange to think about."

"I agree. This is hard to imagine, but I have an even stranger notion for you to ponder.

Another famous thinker of the last century, Max Planck, the Nobel Prize-winning father of quantum theory, wrote, 'All matter originates and exists only by virtue of a force... We must assume behind this force a conscious and intelligent Mind. This Mind is the matrix of all matter."

"Intriguing. So, it seems that we are not as solid as we think we are. There really might be a way for me to impact those at the other end of the world with my thoughts. Honestly, I'll have to think about this more at another time. This is groundbreaking stuff, you know."

"Oh yes, I agree. Well, do you want to do it now?"

"Do what?"

"Comfort them."

"You mean those people in trouble at the other end of the world?"

"Yes, of course."

"And you think I can do that?"

"Do you have an imagination?"

"Yes, of course, but right here and now?"

"You know my opinion. There is no time like the present."

"Will you help me with it?"

"Certainly. First of all, I want you to feel the doubt that says, 'I don't know if I can do it, and I don't even know if it works.' Can you feel that?"

"Oh, yes, definitely."

"So, first of all, feel it without thinking more thoughts or picturing any situations. Just feel the doubt. Then imagine holding this doubt like you were holding the little baby you were. Maybe this doubt baby self is grey.

"Now love him. Hold him tenderly and love him. Comfort him. Love him as much as you are able to love someone. After a while, you will not feel doubt but love. Let me know when that happens."

* * *

"Well, how is it?"

"Better. It almost feels like everything good can happen."

"Is that a good feeling, or what? Do you like it?"

"Yes, absolutely!"

"Now, please bring your energies even more up to speed and love the little baby you truly were —not the grey doubt baby—and let me know when you feel very good."

* * *

"How do you feel now?"

"Even better."

"Now, mentally picture a group of people in the area of the catastrophe and imagine yourself next to them. Imagine smiling at them, talking to them, and comforting them. I also would like you to see them smiling back at you, even if only for a short moment. Let me know when you are done."

* * *

"Done."

"Now, I want you to love them as you love your little baby self. Love them with all your heart. Love them all together or one by one, whatever you feel is best. Just love them."

* * *

"You're smiling. You can do it, right?"

"I am surprised. Yes, I can feel love for them."

"Now I want you to see them in happier circumstances. Imagine their houses being built better than ever. See their children playing happily. See them at suppertime, enjoying good food. See them well dressed and in beautiful surroundings. Imagine the best life for them."

"What is the best life for them?"

"Stretch your imagination. Do your best. Your good intention is all you need here. They will figure out for themselves what they will do with the good energies you send them."

"That makes me feel modest somehow."

"At another time, it will be them who send you good energies. For now, use your great gift of imagination. Trust in the process and do your best."

* * *

"Well, it took you quite some time. How do you feel?"

"I feel like I have some unknown friends somewhere."

Chapter 7

The Ocean of Well-Being

"Ever since we began talking, my life has changed for the better. Nowadays I feel more at ease most days, except for today. I'm having the kind of day where almost everything goes wrong. I feel like I want to jump out of my skin."

"Would you like to feel better?"

"Of course!"

"Let me introduce you to the Ocean of Well-Being."

"Ocean of Well-Being? Is this a visualization, or what?"

"The way you say visualization sounds as if you find it silly or futile."

"Well, I don't want to hurt your feelings, but when I imagine something and pretend it's real, is that not a bit silly?"

"Oh, you really think so? Very interesting! So you are saying that if we make something up in our minds and think it's real, that's bogus?"

"It is not real; I mean not really real like a chair or a tree, right?"

"True, you can't touch it or take a photo of it. You can't put it in your drawer. But this is also true for love. You can't put love into a drawer. But I ask you, does love exist? Does friendship exist? Do loyalty, freedom, and creativity exist?"

"There is a difference. Love, freedom, and creativity exist already. I don't have to make them up in my mind."

"So, some things like love, freedom, and creativity that can't be touched and seen are real, but other things like plans and ideas that we have are not? If, for example, you come up with a good idea and you go to the next meeting at work and say, 'Listen, guys, I have a solution for this problem,' is that a real solution or not?"

"If they follow that lead and make the change, then it is something real."

"What, in your opinion, makes it real?"

"The result."

"Interesting. What do you think when a visualization has results? Is it then real in your opinion?"

"Yes, the result is real."

"Do you agree that the result would not exist if you had not created a solution or other intangible in your mind earlier?"

"I never looked at it that way, but you have a point here. Now please tell me all about this Ocean of Well-Being."

"Okay. Get ready then. Close your eyes and get comfortable in your chair. I want you to listen, see, and feel with your inner senses."

This ocean is vast and bright and has every color you can imagine. It is denser than air but not as dense as water.

You can easily drift in it, gently up or down, or left or right. You can also just stay there as if lying on a cloud. You can breathe it in and out.

You can fill your whole body with the substance of the Ocean of Well-Being. It feels good, this Ocean of Well-Being. So vast, so free, so joyful. It goes on forever and ever.

Drifting so freely through these bright sparkling colors, breathing in and drinking in this freedom and well-being feels so good.

* * *

"Wow. That does feel good. For a while I was really there. Funny that I say 're-ally' after our discussion about what is

real and what isn't. Anyway, it felt real enough for a moment.

"I wish I could feel that good more often. Right now I feel good, but I can get angry so quickly, and I can't always love my anger baby or drift in the Ocean of Well-Being in the middle of my workday. What do I do then?"

"Over time, you learn another way of thinking. Rome was not built in a day. In the future, when you start to get angry, just relax and think, 'Ah, here is this old program again.' And when you think of it this way, you step out of it. You might still be angry to a certain degree, but you don't identify with the anger any longer. It is just another program running in your inner computer, a program that you are modifying day by day because you are tired of it and you want to feel good instead."

"This sounds as if I can be in control of what I feel."

"Certainly. Who else if not you?"

Chapter 8

Small Children and Freedom of Choice

"I now understand how to create happier relationships. This is not only a nice idea, but it is a real option, something that is doable and that everyone, even me, can experience.

"I am glad that I met you and have learned how to build better relationships. Since I have made these changes in me, I feel different: kinder, gentler, and happier. Of

course, I understand that I have to prac-
tice and live it. I will do it.

"There is, however, something that both-
ers me. When I look around at people in
my life, it saddens me that there is so much
heartache. It seems that people hardly
get along even though they seem to be
good people and have good intentions.
Are they happy in their relationships?
Not really. Some are lonely. Some feel
lonely even though they live with a part-
ner or with family. It seems they are missing this sense of kindness, understanding,
friendship, and joy that I now feel in my
life thanks to our conversations and the
changes I've made.

"How can they learn it? Who will teach
them? People should naturally know how
to live in harmony with each other. Why

is this missing in our make-up? Why don't we have this important ability?

"Why are we not happy to begin with?"

"When we are born, we begin to drift like droplets in this enormous ocean on planet Earth called humanity. Millions and billions of these drops make up humanity. They think their thoughts; they feel their emotions; they act or rest.

"It seems as if every drop of this ocean of humanity has its own density and temperature. Some are clearer; some are muddier. A few of them shine like liquid crystals. Others are darkish-opaque. They have different sounds, tastes, and scents. Everyone has their own energy signature.

"Although you come into this life with great expectations, you can become overwhelmed with the noise of all the thinking and feeling around you. These many sounds, colors, and scents have an influence on you, and you on them, of course. The greatest influence comes from your parents, siblings, neighbors, and so on.

"Many of these thoughts and emotions that influence you are sad, angry, or fearful. Although you have just arrived, you feel them. You know what is going on around you. From early on, many of us start vibrating with these emotional energies.

"We adjust to the others and become similar in sound and color to those surrounding us, although they are different from our own vibrations. As we adjust to the energies of others, we are not in harmony with who we truly are. That's why we are oftentimes not happy to begin with."

"You said 'from early on.' You don't mean

very young babies, do you? They can't think from day one of their lives, right?"

"When you look at a baby, or at a woman or a man or a dog or a tree, for that matter, what you see, hear, and touch is only the package. Inside the package is more. Inside is something that you can't see with your eyes, hear with your ears, or touch with your hands. This something is vibrating energy, conscious energy, and, of course, this vibrating conscious energy that we are is able to think and to feel.

"A baby does not need to know words or grammar in order to think. Thinking, feeling, and processing information happens from the beginning. Language comes later."

"When the people around us are sad or angry, we as small babies feel it and start becoming sad and angry ourselves?"

"We are influenced by other people's thoughts and emotions right from the start."

"So we have nothing to say on this matter? We are just the products of our environment, acting out what happens around us with no freedom of our own? That is terrible."

"Oh, you are free alright. You are free whether you know it or not. You are free whether you want it or not. You are truly free to think, feel, and imagine what you want."

"But still, it seems so unjust that so many little ones grow up in an environment where people feel bad and that consequently these children learn to feel bad. Their families are responsible. Parents have to make sure that their baby feels good. It is their duty. And

what about love? They have to love their baby. If not, when will their baby ever be able to feel love?"

"Even as babies, we are able to generate love and good emotions ourselves."

"Come on! Small babies, lying around helplessly, depending on others for food and shelter and cleanliness and everything else, are supposed to create happiness in themselves? How could they possibly do that? Making them happy is the responsibility of the family they are born into."

"What happens if their family is unable to love and to feel good about themselves? Don't you think that there must be something in us, an innate ability that enables us to create happiness and love for ourselves regardless of others?"

103

"That sounds good, but what could that innate ability be?"

"Remember that the energy signature that you are is always and forever. It enables you to think and to feel. You can choose what to think and what to feel. You can choose to feel good or you can choose to feel bad. That is your freedom."

"But isn't it difficult for a child, let alone a newborn baby, to choose what to think and feel?"

"Not more difficult than for adults like you or me."

"This is all so new to me. I am confused. Can you give me an example?"

"Some years ago, I met a young man at a meditation retreat. Let's call him Bill. At dinner he told me his story, which I still remember. It impressed me so deeply.

"Bill grew up in the slums of Chicago. His family lived in a crowded place with many others. Food was scarce. His parents were nice enough, but at times the small amount of money they got from welfare went to alcohol, and when his parents were drunk, they beat him and his siblings. Afterwards, when his parents sobered, they would apologize and cry.

"At the age of seven, Bill decided that he wanted a better life. Now, it is good to make such a decision, however, the next step has to follow, or nothing will change."

"What is the next step? What did the boy do?"

"Something that I admire about him. He did not judge his parents. He did not pity himself. He did not mill over in his mind all the dreadful things that had happened around him. That was wise because thinking about and feeling poverty, sadness, and fear existing all around him would have glued him to the same life circumstances. Remember, what you have in your mind is what you attract into your life experience. The energies you send out—thoughts, and particularly emotions—come back to you.

"Instead of thinking about poverty, sadness, and fear, he thought of something else. He found a hiding place where he would daydream about how he wanted his life to be. He wanted to be a banker like a banker he had seen on TV with a three-piece suit, a briefcase, and a red convertible BMW.

"He daydreamed about it over and over, and

enjoyed it. Also, unlike his siblings, he went to school regularly, paid attention in class, did his homework diligently, and become a good student because a banker would have been a good student, right?

"One day, when one of the school's benefactors asked for an excellent student to promote, Bill was chosen. He was sent to a private school, then to a prestigious college, and eventually he became a banker with three-piece suits, a briefcase, and a red convertible BMW.

"'As an adult, I really don't need a red convertible BMW,' he told me. 'I would be happy with any other decent car. I only got the BMW to fulfill the promise I had made to the little boy I was.'

"Wow! Impressive story! But this boy was already seven years old. It must be differ-

ent with babies, right? Babies are not yet able to make decisions."

"Whether we are babies or adults, we are learning and expanding—if we want to. As babies or as adults, we have the ability to become aware of the love within us and the love surrounding us. Even if there is not much love from our families, there is always love from the divine."

"Well, I'll have to wrap my mind around that for a while. I can't help thinking how much happier I would be if my parents had understood this or if they had been happier themselves! Too bad."

"Not really. It is **now** that you understand more about happiness; it is **now** that you are aware of your choices. All you have to do is make good choices **now**."

"What good choices do you have in mind?"

"The choice to be happy. The choice to open your heart. The choice to appreciate your life. The choice to become quiet and feel, love, and transform the old negative energies. This leads to beginning the life you really want to live."

"Sounds great! Now, coming back to babies—even they can love and feel good, and so they can have a good life, right?"

"Absolutely! Isn't that good news?"

Chapter 9

The Golden Gate

"We talked about choices. For example, that we can make the choice to be happy. But how can we be happy when so many people around us are unhappy?"

"Some things in our world are pretty messy, I have to admit. But what approach is more helpful and more courageous—to lament or to start fresh?"

"How can we make a fresh start? Within our own government there are so many conflicts, and it only gets more complicated when you think of the relationship between different countries. Even within most families, people don't get along."

"Oh no, I don't look for governments or organizations to save us. The fresh start begins with every one of us. Every day a little kinder. Every day a little happier. Every day some moments of stillness. Every day just a little more gratitude. Can you imagine how this will eventually change us and the world we live in?"

"That could be a huge change."

"So, let's start."

"Let's start? How?"

"With the Golden Gate. Imagine that every time you change direction there will be two gates in front of you."

"Change direction—what do you mean by that?"

"When you wake up in the morning, for example, you become aware of your body, your bed, the temperature in the room, and how you feel."

"You mean how my body feels?"

"Yes, and your emotions. Now, some people wake up and feel good. Their body is like a happy cat curled up comfortably. They stretch and yawn and open their eyes, ready to start a good day."

"That doesn't happen to me. When I wake up, I feel lousy. I wish I could just draw

the blanket over my head and go back to sleep."

"Why is that?"

"I think of all the work that waits for me in the office, my lousy commute, and the boring meeting at 10:00 a.m. Not a lot of pleasure, I assure you."

"Aha! Here we have it."

"What 'aha'? Isn't this normal?"

"Normal, maybe, but not natural. What kind of life is it if you start your day already frustrated? Anyway, this waking up scenario is a good example. This is a moment where you can change direction. First of all, things are as they are, no value or feeling attached to them. But very quickly we give meaning to a situation or circumstance.

"When you wake up and start thinking of the day you could be neutral. And some people manage to stay neutral. Facts are facts, circumstances are circumstances. But for many of us, judging kicks in and you have two main choices: to be frustrated or to happily anticipate the day to come. These are the two gates that you have in front of you: The Dark Gate and the Golden Gate.

"You can imagine that the Dark Gate looms in front of you and exudes a feeling of dread. As you open it, you look at the landscape of your life, and it is grey and dreary. Imagine that as you walk through it, dark ink rains down on you.

"The Golden Gate, however, is inviting. As you open it, you glimpse an alternative landscape for your life that is luscious, colorful, and filled with sunshine. As you walk through the gate, imagine golden light softly pouring down on you, filling you with bright energy.

"These are the two gates that are always in front of us: the Dark Gate and the Golden Gate. Every moment we have choices, and what we choose determines the quality of our life.

"So, in the morning when you think of the day ahead, it would be wise to walk through the Golden Gate and look at your work through happy eyes."

"I am not sure if I understand you correctly. These gates, are they metaphors for the choices we have?"

"In a way, yes, but there is more to them. When you use your creative mind to envision these gates in front of you and make the choice to walk through one of them, you will be aware of either becoming enriched with energy or depleted of it."

"Hey, that is unfair! Why do you suggest

that the Dark Gate would deplete me of energy?"

"Take it easy. I just want to describe how your choices have an impact on you.

"Remember, this is about creating change. You want to change something in your life, right? Right now, we are working on changing how you think of and anticipate your day. And by the way, I don't *suggest* that walking through the Dark Gate would deplete you of energy. It is a fact. If you have a sense of boredom or foreboding of something to come, you definitely deplete yourself of energy.

117

"On the other hand, if you make a choice to walk through the Golden Gate, you become more aware of a stream of well- being flowing to you. This enriches you with golden energy. Would you like to try it out?"

"I guess... Sure, why not?"

"So, what are the two directions in front of you right now?"

"I don't know. Nothing comes to mind. Maybe how I feel about the weather? When I look out of the window and see how hard it's raining, I begin to feel frustrated with the rain."

"Good example. Rain is just rain. No need to be frustrated about it but, yes, the judging kicks in. So, please close your eyes and become aware of your choices. Envision the two gates in front of you—the Dark Gate and the Golden Gate.

"Look through the Dark Gate and you will see the landscape of your life as grey and dreary. Walk through the Dark Gate and feel dark ink raining down on you. This feeling goes along with thoughts like 'this nasty weather,' and 'I hate getting wet,' and 'life is difficult.'"

"Exactly."

"Since you don't want to feel this way, please go back and look through the Golden Gate. Here the landscape of your life is filled with golden light even though it is raining. The grey sky seems to shine. The thoughts that come to mind are maybe 'we need this rain for plants and animals,' and 'glad I have an umbrella,' and 'life is good.' Walk through the Golden Gate and feel the bright energy flowing down on you."

* * *

"How do you feel?"

"Good. I would not have thought that this Golden Gate thing could make me feel so good. Is that what you want me to do? To envision these gates every time I need to make a choice? That takes too long. I have much to do, and time flies by fast enough as it is."

"At the beginning, it might take a second or two. When you have done it several times, you will quickly become aware of these gates, like a flash of two images."

"But still it's difficult. That means that I have to stop myself and think about my choices. Even trying to be aware of those choices is a hassle."

"Since we have talked about the two gates, you already have them in your mind. And since you went through the Dark Gate and the Golden Gate, you also have a feeling for them.

"From now on, these options will come to your mind briefly and as swiftly as a swallow flies. You decide which way to go, and if you make a good choice, you feel good."

"You think this is important? Why?"

"We're talking about the life you want, right? Whether you are aware of it or not, every moment you make minute changes in one direction or another.

"Oftentimes, people follow the beaten path and rehash old memories over and over. Instead of creating bright, happy moments that they enjoy, they reproduce dull moments that they have experienced before.

"Now that you are aware of these changes and choices, you are more in control of your life than before. These moment-to-moment changes eventually lead you to a brighter life or a duller life. If you want a bright life, you better walk in its direction."

"Do you really think I can do it?"

"By all means! Just be gentle with yourself as you learn something new. Please remember that you have the choice to live the life you really want to live. It's all about choices. Just make up your mind to be happy. You are able to make the right choices."

"Because I am free."

"Yes. Feels good to be free, right?"

"Absolutely!"

Chapter 10

Is Life Fair?

"Do you think life is fair?"

"What do you mean? Could you be a bit more specific?"

"One of my friends...no, the man is not even a friend of mine, just someone I know, inherited a lot of money recently—and it annoys me."

"Why does it annoy you?"

"This man does not deserve such good luck. He is often rude and a cheapskate. He never invites any of us to dinner but makes sure that he is always on our invite list. He is also a know-it-all and hypocrite. He just gets on my nerves!"

"Please correct me if I am wrong, but are you saying that just because you don't like this man you think it is unfair that he received the inheritance?"

"When you say it this way, it sounds so mean. In general, I wish everyone well, but it annoys me that this pompous cheapskate received such a windfall when more generous, kinder people continue to struggle in life. That is not fair."

"Fair is perhaps not the best word for it, but, yes, I think that life is fair."

"You call this fair? This guy who is so rude and egotistical inherits more than half a

million dollars when a friend of mine, who is so kind and caring and has four little kids, can hardly make enough money to pay his bills. Is that what you call fair?"

"If you had a say, what would fairness look like?"

"Well, the way I see it, the kind and good people should have more money than the mean people."

"Who would decide upon the goodness and the meanness of people?"

"A kind of higher force."

"And this higher force would say you are so good that no matter what you are thinking, planning, or doing you get a hundred thousand dollars every year. And, you lousy creature, you have been so mean, arrogant, and bad you only get enough money to barely live on. Is that what you have in mind?"

"When you put it this way, it sounds so mean. But you must admit that the principle is good."

"Must I? Do you think that there should be a higher force watching us and judging us?"

"Of course, there is! Haven't you been to church lately?"

"Can I ask you to imagine something? Think of good and loving parents who have several children, and these children are all different.

"Some are gentle and some are harsh; some are helpful and some are lazy; some are playful, and some are serious; some like to laugh, and some like to complain. Can you imagine these different children? Now, tell me, how should the parents treat their children?"

"Maybe they should be nicer to the kids who are helpful and happy."

"Now imagine, please, that those kids who are more helpful are also those who like to complain, and the kids who are lazy are the ones who like to laugh."

"So are you saying that helpful children are also those who complain?"

"Not specifically. What I am trying to help you understand is that we are not either all good or all bad. Haven't you noticed that we usually have some of all qualities? But that is not the point here. Should those good and loving parents be good to only some of their children, and if so, to which ones? And should they be less loving to their other children?"

"No, I think that good parents should love all of their children, no matter how the children are and what they do. At least, that is how I would like it to be."

"Why would you like that?"

"All children should be loved. We all need love."

"I agree. Now, please imagine the Source of All Life, this loving infinite magnificent being that many call God. Could you imagine that this Source of All Life could be less loving than good and loving human parents who would love all of their children?"

"Put that way, I agree: no judgment and no punishment. This Source of All Life, as you call it, loves us even more than we are able to love. But shouldn't there be another force, a neutral force so to say, which makes sure that we all get what we should have?"

"We have this force, the universal Law of Resonance, which says 'What you put out is what you get back.'"

"I remember that we talked about it, but I don't know exactly how that works. Please help me out here. It seems that my stingy friend thinks of money all the time, so he always has enough money and even inherits money, right?"

"Right."

"But my poor friend with the small children also seems to think about money all

the time, at least he talks about it a lot. Why doesn't he have enough money?"

"The question is, does your poor friend think about **having** money or of **not having** money?"

"Good question. Now that I think about it, he complains a lot about not having enough money. Ah, I see. Since he thinks about not *having money, he doesn't have much money.*

That's how it works, right? Please correct me if I'm wrong. When I, or anyone else, think of having enough money, I attract

more money. And when I think of not *having enough money, I attract lack of money. So that means that I'm really in charge. That's cool! And I don't need to make it happen; that Universal Law makes it happen. And my part is what again?"*

"To think about what you want and feel good about it. The way you feel is very important."

"But what if I don't feel good about it? What do I do then? Wait! I know. I love my baby self. When I love my baby self that means I love myself. When I love myself, I feel good, which means that I vibrate with high positive energies. The universe reacts to that, and by the Law of Resonance, I experience the good stuff."

"Well said! You are a good student."

"Thank you. I really think I'm getting there."

Chapter 11

Promise

"When you say that I am doing fine, you mean it, don't you?"

"Yes, you can be sure of that. You have been willing to follow me and open your mind and heart to new thoughts and experiences. In fact, I would say that you have been quite courageous."

"Courageous? I never thought of myself as courageous."

"Oh, yes, you are. It takes courage to face your own worries and insecurities and to make changes. You did this. You should be proud of yourself. Thank you for coming along with me so far."

"Wait a minute! This sounds like a fare-well. You are not ending this conversation with me, are you?"

"I am."

"But I have so many more questions!"

"There will be more conversations and more questions answered. We will meet again, if you wish."

"Are you leaving me now?"

"Not really. Look at it this way: People who connect in a sincere and loving way will always stay connected. Also, you know that we can have many friends."

"Right. I remember. I could even have unknown friends somewhere."

"That feels good, doesn't it?"

"Yes, you're right. It feels good to have friends."

"And to be your own best friend."

"I think I'm getting there. I mean, being my own best friend. And yours! By all means, I want to be your friend, too."

"And I yours."

"Promise?"

"Promise."

Brigitte Novalis

"Thank you for being in my life."

"Thank you, too."

About the Author

Boston-based therapist and Reiki Master Brigitte Novalis inspires readers across the world to live their best life (*The Life You Want*) and to find their magical connection with nature (*The Magic of Inner Silence*). Her beautifully illustrated fairy tales enchant both children and grown-ups alike.

Brigitte loves her family, her dogs and cats, Dvorak's Slavonic Dances, and good stories (both reading and writing them!).

In Brigitte's new adventures series, you will follow Anna to the Quentin Academy of Magical Arts and Sciences (*Anna and the Missing Child*), (*Anna and the Mysterious Twins*) and enter a new world where living becomes magical.

You can connect with Brigitte online here:

brigittenovalisbooks.com

Thank you for reading this book. I hope you enjoyed it.

Feedback is an author's lifeblood. If you have a few moments to leave a review on Amazon or Goodreads, even if it's only a couple of lines, I'd be most grateful.